Learn with Alex and Anna

Hello! We're Alex and Anna. That's us with our dog, Freddie. The rest of our family are Grandpa and Grandma, Auntie Lucy, and Mummy and Daddy.

We've been really busy doing lots of fun activities, and we wanted to share some of them with you, so Grandpa decided to write about them.

We have learnt lots of useful things from a number of people. And, Freddie has often been there to lend a helping paw too. We've had so much fun that none of it really felt like learning at all. We welcome you to our books and stories and hope that through this book, you will have just as much fun too.

We ask you to read this story carefully because, at the end of every book, there are some questions for you to answer. Some books may have activities or experiments for you to carry out, as well.

We want to thank you for getting this book and hope you enjoy reading it.

Have fun; we did.

Alex and Anna

Copyright © 2015 Peter Hayward
www.learnwithalexandanna.com

ISBN 13: 978-1508601920

All rights reserved. No part of this publication may be reproduced, distributed, or transmitted in any form or by any means, including photocopying, recording, or other electronic or mechanical methods, without the prior written permission of the publisher or the author, except in the case of brief quotations embodied in critical reviews and certain other non-commercial uses permitted by copyright law.

Peter Hayward asserts the moral right to be
identified as the author of this work.

www.learnwithalexandanna.com

Acknowledgement

I'd like to say a very big thank you to Julie Day, my editor. Without her tremendous help, I know that this book would have fallen well short of the quality the children and parents reading them deserve.

I'd also like to thank Michael Barton, Business Content Creation Limited, for his encouragement, advice, and tireless assistance. Taking a vision and making it reality was a journey along a winding road. Michael helped to straighten it.

This book is dedicated to my grandchildren, Ashley, Lilly, and Emily. Life with them is truly inspiring.

Cars were crashing everywhere! One was tearing around at speed, and another was hurtling into the air, while others were turning on their sides. Today, nobody was safe on the roads.

Actually, this wasn't a real scene, nor was it a film on TV. It was Alex playing with his toy cars.

Anna was also in the room, but she was sensible. She was watching from behind the safety of her toy box.

Meanwhile, Grandpa and Daddy had been outside to check their cars. They were responsible for the safety of everyone carried in them, and they had tested the seatbelts to ensure they were all working properly.

Now, they were sitting at the kitchen table, enjoying a nice mug of coffee with some biscuits. Freddie, the dog, was also with them. His eyes were fixed firmly on the biscuits.

Hearing the din, Daddy said, "Alex, not all cars drive so fast. And, not all cars crash."

"Yes, they do," Alex stated firmly.

"If they did, everyone would get injured," Daddy replied. "Try playing with them nicely – and quietly."

"Okay, Daddy," Alex assured him, not really having much intention to play nicely with his cars – what a silly idea!

Grandpa smiled at Daddy and said, "I remember saying exactly the same to you when you were that age."

"Well, like father, like son," Daddy laughed.

Grandma suddenly appeared in the doorway with Auntie Lucy and said, "Alex, Anna, time to pack all your toys away if you want to come to the park. Freddie, you're coming too."

Alex and Anna loved going to the park with Grandma and Auntie Lucy, and they tidied up as fast as they could.

Freddie also loved going to the park, and he loved biscuits so, now he was in a quandary. His eyes flicked between Alex and Anna getting ready and the biscuits.

'Food or fun?' Freddie mumbled to himself.

It was a hard choice, but the fun of going to the park to chase squirrels up trees won the day, and he was ready in a flash.

When they were outside, Grandma opened the rear hatch of the car, and Freddie jumped in. Here, he had his own doggy space with a pet barrier to keep him safe. The guardrail stopped him from being thrown into the rear seats if the car had to stop suddenly.

Meanwhile, Alex opened the rear door and hopped in. Sitting on his booster chair, he pulled the seatbelt across his shoulder. At the same time, Auntie Lucy opened the opposite door, and Anna climbed in and sat in her child seat.

"Why do we have to wear seatbelts?" Alex asked, fiddling with the buckle.

"Seatbelts, keep us safe and secure when we're in the car," Auntie Lucy replied while securing Anna's seatbelt. "They prevent us from getting hurt if the car has to stop suddenly."

"Why can't I sit in Alex's seat?" Anna asked, fidgeting around in her chair.

"Well, Anna," Auntie Lucy began, "you are younger and

smaller than Alex, so you have to sit in this special chair. This chair keeps you secure and prevents you from slipping out. When you get older and taller, you will also have a seat like Alex's."

Auntie Lucy tugged Anna's seatbelt to ensure it was secure. Then she checked Alex's seatbelt. Satisfied that Alex and Anna were safe, Auntie Lucy sat in the front passenger seat and fastened her seatbelt.

With seatbelts secure and doors closed and locked, Grandma carefully drove off.

"Grandma!" Alex smirked. "Why aren't you driving as fast as my toy cars?"

"I'm driving with care because there are lots of houses here," Grandma replied.

"But, you can still drive fast," Alex urged.

"Lots of houses mean lots of children and animals, and they don't all know about road safety," Grandma explained.

Just then, a car came racing around a corner in the opposite direction. A cat, minding its own business, crawled out from under a parked lorry right in front of the oncoming car. The startled cat darted across the road, causing the car to screech to a halt. After a few seconds, the car drove off again, this time, much slower.

"That was close," Anna screamed.

"It was close," Grandma responded. "That's why I'm driving at a safe speed."

"Not like that car," Alex understood, "which was travelling much too fast."

"That's right," Grandma replied. "It's important to drive carefully in built-up areas. And when it's wet or icy, or even foggy, a driver has to take even more care."

"Do they?" Alex probed.

"They do," Auntie Lucy joined in. "To get a driving licence, people have to learn about road safety and pass a test."

"Yes," Grandma agreed, "and part of a driver's responsibility is to drive at the correct speed whichever road they are on. That's why I'm driving slowly."

"So, you are protecting us?" Alex queried.

"Yes, I am," Grandma replied. "By driving carefully, I'm keeping us all safe."

"And Freddie," Anna shouted out.

'*Yes, and me,*' Freddie mumbled from behind his barrier.

"And other animals and people using the roads, don't forget," Auntie Lucy added. "Grandma is driving slowly in case a child suddenly runs out in front of us."

Unexpectedly, a football flew over a garden hedge and bounced right in front of Grandma's car. A group of children immediately raced into the road after their ball. The youngsters suddenly saw Grandma's car and froze.

Grandma slammed on the brakes and promptly stopped, causing everyone to jolt forward in their seats. Freddie wasn't concentrating and bumped into the guardrail – at least he didn't roll into the rear seat on top of Alex and Anna. And thank goodness

Grandma didn't have anything loose on the seat either. Anything not secured could have become a dangerous flying object.

"Whoa!" Alex gasped.

"Alex! Anna! Are you okay?" Auntie Lucy asked, instantly turning to check on them.

They were both shaken but not hurt.

"Thank goodness I was driving slowly," Grandma warned. "Any faster, and I would have knocked those children over."

"And if we weren't wearing seatbelts, we could have got injured too," Auntie Lucy insisted. "That's why we should *always* wear seatbelts. Seatbelts certainly kept us all out of danger."

"Well done, Grandma," Alex praised. "When I grow up, I'm going to drive slowly near houses too."

"Good," Grandma remarked. "Before Grandpa retired, he worked as a police officer. It was very distressing for him when he arrived at road crashes to find adults or children injured or killed."

"It was distressing for him," Auntie Lucy confirmed. "Grandpa also told me about some adults and children getting injured or killed because they weren't wearing seatbelts."

"I'm always going to wear a seatbelt," Alex claimed.

"So am I," Anna agreed.

"Well done," Grandma praised.

While they were stationary, Auntie Lucy checked Alex and Anna's seatbelts to make sure they were still secure.

Grandma waited until the kids were safely on the footpath

with their ball, and then she carefully drove away.

"Alex and Anna, can you see that dial on the dashboard?" Auntie Lucy asked, pointing to the speedometer.

"Yes," they replied in unison.

"Well, that dial tells us how fast we are going," Auntie Lucy revealed. "Grandma needs to keep under thirty miles per hour. You keep an eye on the dial for a little while and warn Grandma if she goes over thirty."

Alex and Anna instantly fixed their gaze on the speedometer. Freddie also zoomed his eyes on the dial. Each time Freddie saw the needle approach the number thirty, he opened his mouth, ready to bark. But, of course, Grandma was a responsible driver and kept under the speed limit.

While Grandma kept her concentration, Alex and Anna soon lost theirs. So, instead, Auntie Lucy helped them to practice their left from their right. Each time Grandma drove around a corner, Auntie Lucy asked Alex and Anna which way they were turning.

Regularly checking the rear-view mirror, Grandma smiled as she noticed Freddie also turning his head to the left and the right. He was just like a nodding-dog on the parcel shelf!

Arriving at the park, Grandma parked her car at the side of the road.

"Well done, Grandma," Alex praised, "you kept under the speed limit all the way."

"Thank you," Grandma replied.

Alex then hurriedly unfastened his seatbelt and tried to get out of the door on his side.

"Alex, don't get out that side," Grandma pleaded. "Wait until Auntie Lucy gets Anna out, then come out the same side."

"But, I can get out my side," Alex stated.

"The child locks are on, so you won't be able to open the door," Grandma cautioned. "It's also too dangerous for you to get out that side."

"Why," Alex asked.

"You'd step into the road," Grandma warned. "It's much safer for you to get out onto the footpath."

"Why?" Alex asked again.

"You might step out in front of a passing car or lorry,"

Grandma advised. "Slide across to Anna's side and get out onto the footpath."

"Okay, Grandma," Alex replied, realising that she was right.

Sliding across the seat, Alex followed Anna out of the door. Just as Alex stepped onto the footpath, a van sped past, close to the door he was trying to open.

"That van was close!" Alex exclaimed. "I could have got hurt. I'm glad you told me to get out of this side."

"I care for you," Grandma explained. "I want you to be safe."

Auntie Lucy opened the back of the car, and Freddie hopped out. Then they all walked into the park.

After a leisurely stroll around the park, they wandered back to the car.

Grandma opened the tailgate, and Freddie jumped in. Freddie was exhausted, having chased loads of squirrels up trees. Snuggling down on his rug, he immediately fell asleep.

Meanwhile, Auntie Lucy opened the rear door, and Alex climbed in. Sliding across, he hopped into his seat. Anna then crawled in and sat down in her special seat.

"Seatbelts on, everyone," Alex shouted.

"I wanted to say that!" Anna sulked.

"You can be in charge of seatbelts next time," Grandma suggested.

"Alex, I'm in charge next time," Anna proudly announced.

Auntie Lucy clipped Anna's seatbelt in and checked that Alex had secured his. Then she climbed into the front passenger seat and fastened her seatbelt.

With seatbelts all securely buckled and doors closed and locked, Grandma carefully drove home.

To keep Alex and Anna occupied, Auntie Lucy played *I-Spy*. Freddie, though, occupied himself by snoring. Loudly!

While carefully driving along the road, Grandma noticed police officers stopping vehicles further ahead.

"My turn," Grandma joined in. "I spy with my little eye … police officers!"

Everyone looked up and saw police officers talking to car drivers. Grandma slowed down, ready to stop.

A police officer directed Grandma to pull to the side of the road. Grandma duly stopped and wound down the window. The officer approached and peered into the car.

"Hello," the officer greeted them brightly. "We're just checking that everyone is wearing seatbelts."

"I've got my seatbelt on," Alex shouted. "So has my sister."

"That's great," the police officer approved. "There have been a lot of accidents recently. People have been getting injured because they weren't wearing seatbelts."

"I'm in charge of seatbelts next time," Anna announced with authority.

"Wow, that's good to hear from such young people," the officer replied.

"We always wear our seatbelts to keep us safe," Anna

informed the officer.

"I can see that you all have your belts on, and your dog is also secure in the back," the officer noted.

"That's Freddie," Alex said proudly. "He looks after us."

Freddie heard his name and woke up with a start. Jumping up, he nearly bumped his head on the roof.

"And that's Alex, and this is Anna," Grandma announced. "They always wear seatbelts in my car."

"That's fantastic," the police officer replied. "We often stop people in cars because they're not wearing seatbelts. At times, children are not wearing seatbelts either."

"I care for my grandchildren," Grandma replied. "Everyone in my car always wears a seatbelt."

"When I'm old enough to drive, I'm going to make sure everyone in my car wears a seatbelt," Alex commented.

"I am as well," Anna agreed.

"That's great to hear," the officer praised, and he waved Grandma on with a smile.

As Grandma drove away, Alex and Anna waved goodbye. The police officer smiled and waved back before returning to his important work of keeping people safe.

Alex and Anna then resumed their game of I-Spy with Auntie Lucy. Freddie, though, settled down and resumed his snoring.

Grandma soon approached a busy road junction with traffic lights. The lights showed red so, Grandma stopped.

In the next lane, the lights were green for vehicles turning right. After a few moments, the green light changed to red. At the same time, a car travelling at speed approached the lights in the right turn lane. With the light changing to red, the car screeched to a halt. The sudden braking sent a passenger tumbling forwards and crashing into the rear of a front seat. Ouch!

"Did you see that?" Auntie Lucy shrieked.

"They should have been wearing seatbelts," Alex said.

"Yes, they should," Anna agreed.

"They are all putting their seatbelts on now," Grandma mentioned. "That passenger has found out the hard way."

"That's why we always have to wear seatbelts," Auntie Lucy reminded Alex and Anna.

The lights soon changed to green, and Grandma drove off.

Continuing their journey, Alex and Anna played I-Spy again, this time searching for people who weren't wearing seatbelts!

They soon arrived home, and all went indoors.

"Did you have a good time?" Daddy asked as they entered the house.

"Yes, we did," Alex replied. "We got stopped by the police."

"Did you?" Daddy responded. "Why was that?"

"To see if we were wearing seatbelts," Alex answered. "And we were."

"That's good," Daddy smiled, knowing that nobody travelled in Grandma's car without a seatbelt.

"Why must you wear seatbelts?" Mummy asked.

"They keep us safe," Alex and Anna answered together.

"Police officers also want you to be safe," Mummy reasoned.

"Do they?" Alex enquired.

"Yes, they do," Grandpa responded. "Police officers play an important role in everyone's lives. Part of their job is to make sure people are safe."

"If you remember," Grandma recalled, "the police officer told us about people not wearing seatbelts and getting hurt in accidents. So, to ensure that we were all safe, the officer was checking to make sure we were wearing our seatbelts."

Alex then remembered the car stopping sharply at the traffic lights and interrupted, "I saw a car brake quickly, and someone in the back fell forwards because they weren't wearing a seatbelt."

"I hope they didn't get injured?" Daddy queried.

"I think they were okay," Grandma confided. "They all put their seatbelts on pretty sharp afterwards."

"Daddy!" Anna sniffled. "I saw a cat nearly getting run over."

"Oh dear me," Daddy answered.

"A car was driving too fast and nearly knocked the cat over," Alex remembered.

"And then some children ran out into the road in front of us," Anna said. "But Grandma was driving carefully and stopped."

"That must have been scary," Daddy responded.

"It was," Anna replied. "But we were wearing seatbelts, so we didn't hurt."

"Well done, Grandma," Daddy applauded.

"I'm going to drive slowly when I'm old enough to drive," Alex added. "And I'll make sure everyone wears a seatbelt."

"I hope you do," Daddy praised. "Well, I'll switch the kettle on and make us all a nice cup of tea."

Everyone knew Daddy's tea was the best but didn't dare tell Mummy!

"Mummy, can I play with my cars?" Alex asked.

"Of course you can," Mummy replied.

While Daddy was making the tea, Mummy sat at the kitchen table with Grandma and Grandpa. Freddie, though, sat on his bed and waited for the biscuits to appear again.

Anna followed Alex into the lounge. Sitting on the sofa to

watch Alex, she waited for the crashing to start.

Alex placed his play mat on the floor, then picked out some of his favourite toy cars.

Making sure that all the passengers had their seatbelts on, Alex gently pushed his cars around. During one journey, he stopped to let children cross the road. On the next trip, he passed a school and slowed down, telling his passengers, "There may be school children about."

Anna was flabbergasted and couldn't believe her eyes. She had never seen her brother driving his cars so slowly.

After a few minutes, Auntie Lucy wondered why Alex was so quiet and walked into the lounge.

Soon though, Alex started to push his cars around the floor

much faster. Grandpa looked at Daddy and smiled.

"Alex, I'm glad you're not crashing the cars this time," Daddy reminded him. "But remember, not all cars travel so fast."

"That's okay, Daddy," Alex replied. "I'm driving along the main road, and I'm keeping under the speed limit."

Auntie Lucy smiled and sat down. Selecting a police car, she started to push it around the play mat.

"Hello, hello, hello," Auntie Lucy said to Alex in a pretend voice. "I'm a police officer. You are a careful driver. And, you are all wearing your seatbelts. Well done."

"Thank you, officer," Alex replied. "Everyone in my car always has to wear a seatbelt. Seatbelt safety is important."

Alex and Anna had both learnt something today.

Learn with Alex and Anna

Hooray, you have just finished this story.

Let's see if you can answer these questions. Several of them require you to remember some of the important information and facts from the story.

1. Why must you wear a seatbelt?

2. Why should children use the correct car seat for their age and size?

3. Why is it important get out of the car onto the footpath?

4. What could happen to animals and objects not kept secure in a car?

An exercise for you.
Always wear a seatbelt when you travel in cars.

Thank you for reading our book and completing these questions.

We have other stories for you to read on different subjects.

Whatever you do, please try to be safe but have fun.

We did.

Don't forget you can find out more at:

www.learnwithalexandanna.com

and

www.facebook.com/learnwithalexandanna

Alex and Anna

Other Books in the Series

Alex and Anna become Rain Molecules

The Trapped Duck

Grandpa's Train Journey

Alex Teaches Road Safety

Chasing Shadows

Anna the Honeybee

My Cupcakes

BBQ Time

A Day at the Beach

Freddie the Wonder Dog

www.learnwithalexandanna.com

www.facebook.com/learnwithalexandanna

Learn with Alex and Anna

The remaining pages have intentionally been left blank for you to do some drawing and colouring or make notes.

Printed in Great Britain
by Amazon